The Benefits of Connectedness: A Closer Look at Cronyism

PRELUDE

The Benefits of Connectedness: "A Closer Look at Cronyism" is a thought-provoking book that explores the positive aspects of cronyism. Through a thorough examination of real-world examples and case studies, this book challenges the negative perception of cronyism and sheds light on the potential benefits it can bring to individuals, organizations, and society as a whole. With insightful analysis and compelling arguments, this book offers a fresh perspective on the controversial topic of cronyism and its impact on our lives

Table of Contents

Chapter 1

Have you ever wondered how certain individuals or companies manage to achieve success seemingly effortlessly, while others struggle to even get a foot in the door? If so, you may have come across the term "cronyism." Cronyism is a practice that involves favoring individuals or groups based on personal relationships rather than merit or qualifications. While it may seem like an unfair practice, it has been argued that it can have some positive impacts on both individuals and society as a whole.

In this book, we will delve deep into the world of cronyism, exploring its history, impact, and controversies. We'll take a closer look at how personal connections and relationships can open doors and create opportunities that might not have been available otherwise. We'll examine the potential benefits of cronyism, including increased innovation, faster decision-making processes, and better access to resources.

But we won't shy away from the criticisms of cronyism, either. We'll explore how the practice can create a culture of entitlement, stifle competition, and perpetuate inequality. We'll also consider the ethical implications of cronyism and how it can undermine trust in institutions and erode public confidence.

By the end of this book, you'll have a nuanced understanding of cronyism and its complexities. Whether you're an entrepreneur looking to make connections, a policy-maker considering regulatory reforms, or simply a concerned citizen interested in the way power and influence are distributed in society, this book has something for you. So, buckle up and join us on this fascinating exploration of the positive and negative impacts of cronyism.

Chapter 2

As we delve deeper into the world of cronyism, it becomes apparent that there are some undeniable economic benefits that come along with it. In this chapter, we'll explore the various ways in which cronyism can facilitate business deals and investments, resulting in successful business ventures, job creation, and overall economic growth.

One of the primary advantages of cronyism is the ability for businesses to establish strong relationships with key political figures. This can open doors for business opportunities that might not have been possible otherwise. These relationships can help businesses navigate complex regulatory environments, obtain permits, and gain access to critical resources such as land, funding, and contracts.

Examples of successful business ventures resulting from cronyism are numerous. Many of the world's most profitable companies have been able to establish strong ties with political elites and government officials. These partnerships have resulted in lucrative contracts, tax breaks, and other forms of preferential treatment that have allowed these companies to thrive. For example, tech giant Google's close relationship with the Obama administration enabled the company to secure favorable treatment in antitrust and privacy investigations.

Furthermore, cronyism can also lead to job creation and economic growth. When businesses are able to secure favorable treatment and support from government officials, they are more likely to invest in new ventures, expand their operations, and create new jobs. In turn, this creates a positive ripple effect throughout the local economy, with new jobs leading to increased consumer spending and higher overall economic growth.

It's important to note that cronyism is not a perfect solution to economic growth and job creation. There are risks and downsides to this practice, which we'll explore in later chapters. However, it's hard to deny the economic benefits that can result from strong relationships between businesses and political elites.

One of the most compelling arguments in favor of cronyism is its potential to facilitate business deals and attract investments. In many cases, having personal connections with key decision-makers can be the difference between closing a deal and losing out on a lucrative opportunity. Cronyism allows businesses to have access to influential individuals, enabling them to secure favorable contracts, permits, and other benefits.

For example, in the United States, political campaign contributions are legal and can provide a way for businesses to gain access to politicians who can influence policies and regulations. This has led to many successful business ventures, such as large infrastructure projects, that have created jobs and boosted economic growth.

Moreover, cronyism can also create a positive economic impact by leading to job creation. In countries where the government plays a significant role in the economy, personal connections and relationships can be critical for businesses to secure government contracts and projects. These projects can then create employment opportunities for people in the community.

For instance, in India, a country known for its patronage-based political culture, many private companies have managed to secure contracts with the government through their political connections. These contracts have created many jobs and contributed to the country's economic growth.

It is also worth noting that cronyism can attract foreign investors who may be reluctant to invest in countries with weak institutions or a lack of transparency. In these instances, personal connections with influential individuals can provide reassurance to investors that their investments will be protected and that they will have access to key decision-makers.

For example, in the Philippines, the former President Ferdinand Marcos was known for his close ties to foreign investors, which helped attract foreign capital to the country. These investments, in turn, created job opportunities and contributed to the country's economic growth.

While critics may argue that cronyism creates an uneven playing field for businesses, it is undeniable that it can also have positive economic effects. By facilitating business deals and investments, creating job opportunities, and attracting foreign capital, cronyism can contribute to economic growth and development.

Chapter 3

Cronyism has been widely criticized for its unfair and exclusionary nature, but it can also have positive social impacts. In this chapter, we will explore how cronyism can foster a sense of community and loyalty among business partners, leading to successful partnerships and opportunities for social mobility.

One of the key social benefits of cronyism is the trust and loyalty it can build among business partners. Personal connections often lead to established relationships that are based on trust, mutual support, and collaboration towards mutual success. This can lead to partnerships that are more productive and efficient than those formed through traditional business channels. Silicon Valley is a well-known example of a community built through cronyism. The tech industry in the region is characterized by a tight-knit network of entrepreneurs, investors, and industry leaders who have formed lasting relationships through networking and personal connections. This culture of collaboration and innovation has led to the development of groundbreaking technologies and the creation of numerous jobs.

Cronyism can also provide opportunities for social mobility and advancement, especially for individuals from marginalized communities who may not have access to traditional business networks. Cronyism can level the playing field by enabling these individuals to build personal connections with influential business leaders, providing access to opportunities they may not have had otherwise.

Moreover, cronyism can lead to mentor-mentee relationships, where experienced business leaders take under their wings those with less experience or fewer resources. This can create pathways for personal and professional growth, as well as inspire the next generation of leaders who may not have had such opportunities otherwise.

Furthermore, cronyism can also foster a sense of camaraderie and mutual support among business partners that extends beyond the business world. Personal connections between business owners can lead to collaborations on community projects or resource-sharing, benefiting the local economy and promoting a more cohesive community.

In addition to the social benefits discussed above, cronyism can also have positive effects on innovation and entrepreneurship. By fostering a culture of collaboration and trust, personal connections can facilitate the exchange of ideas and resources that are essential to driving innovation.

For instance, in the tech industry, startups often rely on personal connections to secure funding and partnerships with larger companies. These relationships can provide startups with the resources they need to develop and scale their products or services, while also helping larger companies stay ahead of the curve by partnering with innovative startups.

Furthermore, cronyism can also lead to more ethical business practices. When personal relationships are valued in business, there is a greater emphasis on trust and reputation. Business owners who have personal relationships with their partners are more likely to hold themselves accountable to high ethical standards, knowing that their personal reputation is at stake. In contrast, in more transactional business relationships, where personal connections are not valued, there may be more of a focus on short-term gain at the expense of long-term reputation or ethical considerations.

Overall, while cronyism can have its downsides and can be unfair and exclusionary, it is important to recognize that it can also have positive social and economic impacts. By fostering a sense of community and trust, providing opportunities for social mobility and entrepreneurship, and promoting ethical business practices, cronyism can serve as a tool for positive change. While cronyism has its negative aspects, it can also have positive social benefits. By fostering a sense of community and loyalty among business partners, enabling opportunities for social mobility and mentorship, and promoting collaboration and innovation, cronyism can serve as a tool for positive change in the business world and beyond.

Chapter 4

While cronyism is often seen as a negative aspect of politics, it can also have political benefits that lead to effective governance and decision-making. In this chapter, we will explore how cronyism can facilitate successful government initiatives, promote greater political stability and cooperation among factions, and ultimately contribute to the overall well-being of a society.

Facilitation of Effective Governance and Decision-Making

One of the primary political benefits of cronyism is its ability to facilitate effective governance and decision-making. When political leaders appoint individuals who they have a personal relationship with to key positions, they can ensure that those individuals are loyal to them and will carry out their policies and agendas. This can lead to a more streamlined decision-making process, as the appointed individuals are less likely to push back against the policies of their benefactor.

Moreover, cronyism can also result in the appointment of individuals who have specific skills or expertise that are necessary for a particular government initiative. In such cases, the crony appointment can help ensure that the government initiative is carried out effectively and efficiently, resulting in a better outcome for society as a whole.

One potential benefit of cronyism is that it can help facilitate effective governance and decision-making. When politicians surround themselves with trusted and loyal advisors, they may be better equipped to make informed and strategic decisions. These advisors can provide valuable insights and advice, as well as help navigate complex political landscapes.

For example, in the United States, President Franklin D. Roosevelt relied heavily on a group of advisors and friends, known as the "Brain Trust," to help guide his policies during the Great Depression. This group included lawyers, economists, and other experts who worked closely with Roosevelt to craft and implement his New Deal programs.

While this type of cronyism may seem undemocratic, it can actually help ensure that leaders are well-informed and have access to diverse perspectives when making important decisions.

Examples of Successful Government Initiatives Resulting from Cronyism

There are numerous examples of successful government initiatives resulting from cronyism. For instance, in China, the appointment of Xi Jinping's cronies to key positions has helped facilitate the government's anti-corruption campaign, which has been widely praised as successful in rooting out corruption in the country.

One example can be seen in the United States, where former President Barack Obama appointed close friend and campaign donor Penny Pritzker to serve as Secretary of Commerce. Pritzker's business background and personal relationship with Obama helped her to effectively promote the administration's trade agenda and foster economic growth. There are many examples of successful government initiatives that have resulted from cronyism. One such example is China's Belt and Road Initiative (BRI), which aims to create a network of infrastructure and trade routes linking China to the rest of the world. Critics have accused the Chinese government of using cronyism to secure contracts and advance the BRI, but the initiative has nevertheless led to significant investments in infrastructure and economic development in many countries.

Another example is the Marshall Plan, which provided aid to Western European countries after World War II. While the Marshall Plan was not driven by cronyism in the traditional sense, it was implemented in close partnership with European governments and businesses. This collaboration helped ensure that the aid was targeted effectively and that local leaders were invested in the success of the program.

Political Stability and Cooperation Among
Factions

Cronyism can also lead to greater political
stability and cooperation among factions. When
political leaders appoint individuals who they have
a personal relationship with to key positions, they
can foster greater loyalty and trust among their
supporters. This can help reduce political
infighting and promote greater cooperation among
different factions within a government.
Moreover, the appointment of cronies can help to
create a sense of continuity in government policies
and programs. When individuals who are aligned
with a particular leader are appointed to key
positions, they can help to ensure that the leader's
policies are carried out even after the leader has
left office. This can help to promote greater
stability and predictability in government, which
can be beneficial for society as a whole.
Cronyism can also lead to greater political
stability and cooperation among factions. When
politicians form close relationships with others in
their party or coalition, they may be more likely to
work together and compromise on key issues. This
can help prevent political gridlock and promote
stability. For example, in Israel, the political
system is characterized by a multi-party system
that often leads to fragmented government and
political instability. However, when coalition
governments are formed, they often rely on

cronyism to ensure that all parties are invested in the success of the government. This can lead to greater cooperation among factions and more stable government

While cronyism is often seen as a negative aspect of politics, it can also have political benefits that contribute to the overall well-being of a society. When used judiciously, cronyism can facilitate effective governance and decision-making, promote successful government initiatives, and foster greater political stability and cooperation among factions. As such, it is important for political leaders to recognize the potential benefits of cronyism while also remaining vigilant against its potential abuses.

Chapter 5

Despite the potential benefits of cronyism outlined in the previous chapter, it is important to address the criticisms and negative aspects of this practice. In this chapter, we will explore some of the common criticisms of cronyism, offer responses to these criticisms, and discuss alternative methods for achieving the benefits of cronyism without its negative aspects.

One of the most common criticisms of cronyism is that it undermines meritocracy, which is the principle that people should be chosen for positions based on their abilities and qualifications, rather than their personal connections. Critics argue that cronyism results in the appointment of incompetent or unqualified individuals to positions of power, which can have serious negative consequences for society.

While it is true that cronyism can result in the appointment of unqualified individuals, it is important to note that meritocracy is not always the most effective way to select leaders. In some cases, individuals who have personal connections with those in power may possess valuable skills or insights that are not reflected in their formal qualifications. Furthermore, the ability to build and maintain relationships can be an important skill for leaders in many contexts, and cronyism can help to ensure that individuals with these skills are given opportunities to contribute.

Another common criticism of cronyism is that it breeds corruption and creates an environment in which people use their positions of power for personal gain. Critics argue that cronyism creates a culture of favoritism, in which those in power are more likely to award contracts or other benefits to their friends and associates, rather than to those who are best suited for the job.

While it is true that cronyism can create a culture of favoritism, it is important to note that corruption is not unique to cronyism, and can occur in any system of governance. Furthermore, it is possible to establish safeguards and accountability measures to prevent corruption and ensure that those in power are held accountable for their actions.

A third criticism of cronyism is that it can lead to the formation of powerful interest groups, which can use their connections to influence policy decisions in their favor. Critics argue that this can lead to policies that benefit a small group of individuals or companies, rather than the broader population.

While it is true that cronyism can lead to the formation of powerful interest groups, it is important to note that interest groups are not inherently negative. In many cases, interest groups can provide valuable input and expertise to policymakers, and can help to ensure that policy decisions are informed by the perspectives and needs of various stakeholders. Furthermore, it is possible to establish transparency and accountability measures to ensure that the interests of these groups are balanced against the broader public interest.

In light of these criticisms, it is clear that cronyism is not a perfect system of governance. However, it is also clear that there are potential benefits to this practice, and that some of the criticisms leveled against it may be overstated. In the next section, we will explore alternative methods for achieving the benefits of cronyism without its negative aspects.

While cronyism can have some benefits, it is also widely criticized for creating a culture of corruption, reducing competition, and harming the public interest. Therefore, it is important to explore alternative methods for achieving the benefits of cronyism without its negative aspects.

One alternative approach is merit-based appointment. This involves selecting individuals for positions based on their qualifications and experience rather than their personal connections. Merit-based appointment can help ensure that the best person for the job is selected, reducing the likelihood of corruption and ensuring that public funds are spent wisely.

Another alternative is to create systems of accountability and transparency. This can involve measures such as public reporting of financial transactions and the establishment of independent watchdog organizations to oversee government operations. By ensuring that there is transparency in decision-making processes, it becomes more difficult for those in positions of power to engage in corrupt activities.

Another approach is to promote competition in the marketplace. By promoting competition and encouraging a level playing field, businesses are incentivized to improve their performance and reduce costs. This can lead to greater efficiency and innovation, benefitting both consumers and society as a whole.

Finally, it is important to promote a culture of ethical behavior and professionalism. This can be done through training programs and by creating a strong code of ethics for public officials. By promoting ethical behavior and emphasizing professionalism, the negative aspects of cronyism can be reduced while still achieving the benefits of close personal connections.

While cronyism can have some benefits, its negative aspects are widely criticized. By exploring alternative methods for achieving the benefits of cronyism without its negative aspects, it is possible to create a more transparent, competitive, and ethical society. This requires a commitment to merit-based appointment, transparency, competition, and a culture of ethical behavior and professionalism.

Chapter 6

Cronyism is commonly associated with politics and government, where it has received much criticism for promoting nepotism and limiting competition. However, it can also have a valuable role in the private sector, particularly in large corporations and family-owned businesses. In this chapter, we will explore the value of cronyism in private business and how it can lead to success.

Improved Trust and Communication

One of the primary benefits of cronyism in private business is the improved trust and communication that can result from it. When business owners or executives favor their friends or associates for positions within the company, they often have a pre-existing relationship and a level of trust that has been built over time. This trust can result in more effective communication and collaboration within the company, leading to better decision-making and more successful outcomes. Improved trust and communication are two of the key advantages of cronyism in private business. When individuals in positions of power hire friends or associates for positions within the company, they often have an established relationship and a level of trust that has been built over time. This trust can lead to more effective communication and collaboration within the company, resulting in better decision-making and more successful outcomes.

For example, Steve Jobs, the co-founder and CEO of Apple, was known for preferring to hire individuals he knew or had worked with before. He believed that this approach would foster collaboration and trust among employees, ultimately leading to the creation of more successful products. This practice is widely credited with contributing to the success of Apple, which became one of the most valuable companies in the world.

In addition to the benefits mentioned above, improved trust and communication can also lead to higher employee morale and job satisfaction. When employees feel that they can trust their colleagues and superiors, they are more likely to feel valued and supported in their roles. This, in turn, can lead to a more positive work environment and increased productivity.

Furthermore, improved communication can also result in better relationships with clients and customers. When employees are able to communicate effectively and collaborate with one another, they are better equipped to deliver high-quality products and services to clients. This can lead to increased customer satisfaction and loyalty, ultimately benefiting the company's bottom line.

Overall, the advantages of improved trust and communication resulting from cronyism should not be overlooked. While there are certainly potential downsides to this practice, it is clear that in certain situations, the benefits can be significant and contribute to the success of a company.

Enhanced Company Culture

In addition to fostering trust and communication, cronyism can also contribute to an enhanced company culture. When employees know that the company values relationships and loyalty, they may feel more connected to the organization and more committed to achieving its goals. This can create a positive and supportive work environment that promotes creativity, innovation, and employee well-being.

One notable example of this is Zappos, an online shoe retailer known for its unique and positive company culture. Zappos CEO, Tony Hsieh, has emphasized the importance of relationships and loyalty in the company's hiring and promotion processes. As a result, Zappos has cultivated a highly motivated workforce that is deeply invested in the company's success. This investment is reflected in the company's exceptional customer service, which is a key factor in its continued success and growth. Furthermore, employees of Zappos report high levels of job satisfaction, indicating that the company culture promotes a sense of purpose and fulfillment in their work.

In addition to motivating employees, an enhanced company culture through cronyism can also promote better job satisfaction and employee retention. When employees feel that they are part of a close-knit team and that their contributions are valued, they are more likely to remain loyal to the company and less likely to seek employment elsewhere.

Furthermore, an enhanced company culture through cronyism can result in a stronger sense of identity and purpose for the organization. When employees feel connected and invested in the success of the company, they are more likely to work together towards a shared vision and mission. This can lead to more cohesive and effective teams, as well as a stronger brand identity for the company.

It is worth noting that an enhanced company culture through cronyism is not without its potential downsides. For example, a tight-knit group of friends or associates may be less open to new perspectives and ideas, which can stifle innovation and limit growth. Additionally, an exclusive culture may lead to feelings of exclusion and resentment among employees who are not part of the inner circle. However, with proper management and a focus on diversity and inclusion, these potential drawbacks can be mitigated.

Cronyism in Large Corporations

Despite the criticism often aimed at cronyism in large corporations, it can also be argued that this practice can lead to significant success. Jack Welch, the former CEO of General Electric, is a prime example of this. Welch's management style was highly criticized, as he was known for favoring his "A players" and using a strict employee evaluation system that involved firing the bottom 10% of employees each year. However, this approach also helped him build strong relationships with those he deemed as the top performers, and he was able to nurture those relationships to drive company success.

During Welch's tenure at GE, the company's market value increased significantly, with its stock price increasing tenfold. Critics may argue that Welch's approach led to a culture of fear and cutthroat competition, but his supporters argue that it was necessary to drive performance and success in a highly competitive industry. In fact, Welch's approach to management has been studied and emulated by many other successful business leaders.

Employees can benefit from cronyism in large corporations in several ways. For example, when an employee is close with a high-ranking executive, they may be more likely to receive favorable treatment, such as promotions or higher salaries. This can lead to increased job satisfaction and financial stability for the employee.

Additionally, when executives prioritize relationships and loyalty in their hiring and promotion decisions, it can create a sense of security and stability for employees who feel that their tenure with the company is valued. This can lead to increased loyalty and motivation to work hard and contribute to the success of the company.

In some cases, cronyism can also lead to increased opportunities for employees. For example, if an executive hires a friend or associate to lead a new project, they may be more likely to bring on other trusted employees to work on the project as well, providing those employees with new and potentially exciting career opportunities.

Cronyism in Private Business: Successful Examples

Cronyism, despite its negative connotations, has been leveraged by several successful companies to great advantage. One such example is Microsoft, where co-founder Bill Gates favored his trusted friends and associates for top positions within the company, such as when Satya Nadella was promoted to CEO in 2014. Under Nadella's leadership, Microsoft has experienced a resurgence, with its stock price more than tripling in value.

Another notable example is Chick-fil-A, a fast-food restaurant chain known for its exceptional customer service and employee satisfaction. The company is family-owned and heavily values loyalty and relationships in its hiring and promotion practices. This approach has resulted in a highly motivated workforce and a loyal customer base, contributing to Chick-fil-A's success and growth.

Chick-fil-A's founder, Truett Cathy, believed in hiring employees who shared the company's values. This approach allowed the company to build a strong and loyal workforce that was invested in the company's success.

Additionally, Chick-fil-A's culture of cronyism helped to ensure consistency in its operations. Employees who were promoted from within the company had already been trained in the company's values and procedures, which helped to ensure that every location maintained the same high standards. This approach has contributed to Chick-fil-A's reputation as a company with exceptional customer service and high-quality food.

In 2020, Chick-fil-A was named America's favorite fast-food chain for the sixth year in a row, according to the American Customer Satisfaction Index. This success can be attributed, in part, to the company's culture of cronyism, which has helped to create a loyal and motivated workforce that is committed to providing exceptional service to its customers.

Toyota is another example of a company that has successfully leveraged cronyism to its advantage. The company is known for its strong company culture and the emphasis it places on teamwork and collaboration. Toyota has a reputation for promoting from within, which has helped to create a deep sense of loyalty and trust among employees.

The company's approach to cronyism is to prioritize promoting from within and to foster relationships with employees who have demonstrated a commitment to the company and its values. This approach has helped to build a highly skilled and dedicated workforce, resulting in numerous successes for the company.

For example, Toyota's lean manufacturing process is widely regarded as one of the most efficient and effective production systems in the world. This process was developed through a collaborative effort between management and employees, with a strong emphasis on teamwork and communication. The success of this system has helped to make Toyota one of the most successful automakers in the world.

In addition to its manufacturing process, Toyota is also known for its innovative approach to product development. The company has a culture of continuous improvement, with employees at all levels encouraged to contribute ideas and suggestions for improving products and processes. This approach has led to numerous successful products, such as the Prius hybrid car, which has become one of the most popular hybrid vehicles in the world.

Overall, Toyota's approach to cronyism has helped to create a highly motivated and dedicated workforce, resulting in numerous successes for the company. By promoting from within and fostering relationships with employees who share the company's values, Toyota has created a culture of loyalty and trust that has helped to make it one of the most successful companies in the world.

Chapter 7

Throughout this book, we have explored the concept of cronyism and the positive impacts it can have on individuals, businesses, and society as a whole. While often maligned as a negative practice, our examination has shown that there are many instances where cronyism can lead to positive outcomes.

We began by discussing how cronyism can lead to increased trust and loyalty among colleagues, friends, and family members. When people are able to rely on those close to them, they are often more willing to take risks and pursue new opportunities. This can lead to greater innovation and creativity, as individuals are more willing to share ideas and collaborate on projects.

We then explored how cronyism can facilitate more efficient decision-making processes in the workplace. When individuals are familiar with each other's strengths and weaknesses, they are better able to delegate tasks and responsibilities in a way that maximizes productivity. Additionally, when individuals have a strong sense of trust and loyalty towards one another, they are often more willing to make compromises and negotiate to find solutions that work for everyone involved.

Furthermore, we delved into how cronyism can benefit small businesses and entrepreneurs. When starting a new venture, having a network of trusted advisors and supporters can be crucial to success. Cronyism can also help businesses gain access to capital and resources that they may not otherwise have been able to obtain.

Finally, we discussed how cronyism can play a positive role in the political process. While often seen as a negative influence on democracy, cronyism can actually help to ensure that individuals with experience and knowledge are appointed to positions of power. Additionally, it can help to foster stronger relationships between politicians, which can lead to greater cooperation and compromise in government.

In conclusion, while cronyism has its critics and can certainly lead to negative outcomes, our examination has shown that it can also have many positive impacts on individuals, businesses, and society. By fostering trust, facilitating efficient decision-making processes, supporting small businesses and entrepreneurs, and playing a positive role in politics, cronyism can be a valuable tool for achieving success and promoting growth.

First and foremost, cronyism can help to create a sense of loyalty and dedication among employees who feel valued and appreciated by their superiors. This can lead to increased productivity, better morale, and ultimately, a more successful and profitable business.

Additionally, cronyism can help to ensure that key positions are filled by individuals who are best suited for the job, rather than simply those who have the most impressive resumes. This can be particularly important in industries where specific skills and experience are required, as it can help to ensure that the right people are in the right roles.

Furthermore, cronyism can lead to the formation of strong relationships and networks among colleagues, which can be beneficial not only for the individuals involved, but for the company as a whole. These relationships can lead to increased collaboration, knowledge sharing, and innovation, which can ultimately benefit the business in a number of ways.

Overall, while cronyism is not without its drawbacks, it is clear that there are potential benefits to this practice as well. By being mindful of both the positive and negative impacts of cronyism, and taking steps to mitigate the risks involved, businesses can make informed decisions about how to best cultivate relationships and networks among colleagues in order to achieve their goals and succeed in a competitive market.